SandCastle™

First Rhymes

Simone
on the Throne

Anders Hanson

Consulting Editor, Diane Craig, M.A./Reading Specialist

ABDO
Publishing Company

Published by ABDO Publishing Company, 4940 Viking Drive, Edina, Minnesota 55435.

Credits
Edited by: Pam Price
Curriculum Coordinator: Nancy Tuminelly
Cover and Interior Design and Production: Mighty Media
Photo Credits: AbleStock, Brand X Pictures, Hemera, Photodisc, Wewerka Photography

Library of Congress Cataloging-in-Publication Data

Hanson, Anders, 1980-
    Simone on the throne / Anders Hanson.
        p. cm. -- (First rhymes)
    Includes index.
    ISBN 1-59679-505-0 (hardcover)
    ISBN 1-59679-506-9 (paperback)
        1. English language--Rhyme--Juvenile literature. I. Title. II. Series.

PE1517.H3785 2005
808.1--dc22

2005048041

SandCastle™ books are created by a professional team of educators, reading specialists, and content developers around five essential components that include phonemic awareness, phonics, vocabulary, text comprehension, and fluency. All books are written, reviewed, and leveled for guided reading and early intervention reading, and designed for use in shared, guided, and independent reading and writing activities to support a balanced approach to literacy instruction.

Let Us Know

After reading the book, SandCastle would like you to tell us your stories about reading. What is your favorite page? Was there something hard that you needed help with? Share the ups and downs of learning to read. We want to hear from you! To get posted on the ABDO Publishing Company Web site, send us e-mail at:

sandcastle@abdopub.com

SandCastle Level: Beginning

3 1561 00181 8040

bone

cone

phone

stone

throne

I look at the .

We look at a  .

We see a  .

This is a  .

I look at the  .

The bone is long.

The cone is good.

This phone is old.

The stone is hard.

The throne is big.

Simone on the Throne

Queen Simone
sits on a throne.

Next to the throne
is a big stone.

On the stone
next to the throne
is a phone.

Queen Simone
sits on her throne
by the stone.

She talks on
the phone
and gives her dog
an ice-cream cone.

The dog sits by
Queen Simone
on her throne
and the stone
with the phone.

He eats the cone,
but wishes it were
a bone!

About SandCastle™

A professional team of educators, reading specialists, and content developers created the SandCastle™ series to support young readers as they develop reading skills and strategies and increase their general knowledge. The SandCastle™ series has four levels that correspond to early literacy development in young children. The levels are provided to help teachers and parents select the appropriate books for young readers.

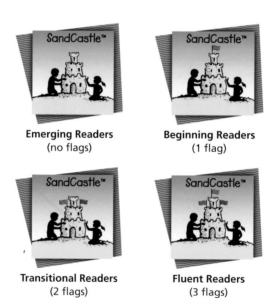

Emerging Readers
(no flags)

Beginning Readers
(1 flag)

Transitional Readers
(2 flags)

Fluent Readers
(3 flags)

These levels are meant only as a guide. All levels are subject to change.

To see a complete list of SandCastle™ books and other nonfiction titles from ABDO Publishing Company, visit www.abdopub.com or contact us at:
4940 Viking Drive, Edina, Minnesota 55435 • 1-800-800-1312 • fax: 1-952-831-1632